Cave Dance
(Snare Drum Solo with Foot Pedal Instrument)

By Glenn Kotche

CW00418079

About the Solo

"Cave Dance" is inspired by flamenco dance performances that I experienced in Málaga, Spain. These dramatic, flamboyant, and virtuosic performances take place in the Sacromonte district caves, which have been converted into Romani entertainment venues.

This piece is derived from recordings that I made featuring various combinations of folk dances strung together into a performance (hence, the constantly shifting tempos and feels that occur within this piece). Some of these dances featured female dancers and some male, some were with instrumental accompaniment, and others were backed with just hand claps or castanets.

The foot pedal instrument (bass drum, cowbell, woodblock or foot stomp) called for in the piece is meant to emulate the frequent and very percussive foot stomps of the dancers, while the rapid stick clicks are meant to evoke those times when the dancers pause awaiting applause from the audience. The parts written to be played on the rim of the snare drum can be substituted for another percussive timbre (closed hi-hat, woodblock, bongo, etc.).

Performance Options

In addition to being played as-is, "Cave Dance" can be performed using two shortcuts as well. The first will require you to skip from the end of measure 52 (the 2/4 rest) to the beginning of measure 66. The second will require you to skip from the end of measure 86 to the beginning of measure 96 (the 2/4 rest).

Legend

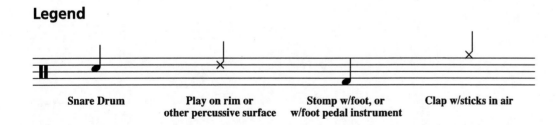

| Snare Drum | Play on rim or other percussive surface | Stomp w/foot, or w/foot pedal instrument | Clap w/sticks in air |

Alfred's PERCUSSION PERFORMANCE SERIES

Cave Dance

Glenn Kotche

SNARE DRUM SOLO
(with Foot Pedal Instrument)

About the Author

Chicago-based percussionist and composer Glenn Kotche has been called one of the most exciting, creative, and promising composers and performers in modern music, receiving international attention for his "unfailing taste, technique, and discipline" (*Chicago Tribune*). After three solo records, including his 2006 album *Mobile* (Nonesuch Records), Kotche will release his fourth studio album in 2013. Kotche has written pieces for world-renowned ensembles including Kronos Quartet, The Silk Road Ensemble, Bang on a Can All-Stars, So Percussion, and Eighth Blackbird.

In addition to his work as a composer and solo percussionist, Kotche is a member of the groundbreaking American rock band Wilco, with whom he has played since 2001. With Wilco, he has recorded the records *Yankee Hotel Foxtrot* and *Kicking Television*, as well as the Grammy-nominated *Sky Blue Sky*, *Wilco (The Album)*, and *The Whole Love*, and the Grammy-winning *A Ghost Is Born*. Beyond Wilco, Kotche records and performs regularly along with Darin Gray in the long time rhythm duo On Fillmore. He is also a member of the trio Loose Fur along with Jim O'Rourke and Jeff Tweedy.

Kotche has appeared twice on the cover of *Modern Drummer* and once on the cover of *Percussive Notes*, the official publication of the Percussive Arts Society of which Kotche is currently a board member. He resides in Chicago with his wife and two children.

glennkotche.com